Need to Know

Cancer

Oliver Gillie

Heinemann
LIBRARY

www.heinemann.co.uk/library

Visit our website to find out more information about **Heinemann Library** books.

To order:

 Phone 44 (0) 1865 888066

 Send a fax to 44 (0) 1865 314091

 Visit the Heinemann Bookshop at www.heinemann.co.uk/library to browse our catalogue and order online.

Produced by Monkey Puzzle Media Ltd
Gissing's Farm, Fressingfield, Suffolk IP21 5SH, UK

First published in Great Britain by Heinemann Library, Halley Court, Jordan Hill, Oxford OX2 8EJ, part of Harcourt Education.
Heinemann is a registered trademark of Harcourt Education Ltd.

Editorial: Clare Collinson
Design: Jamie Asher
Picture Research: Sally Cole
Consultant: Louise Soanes
Production: Viv Hichens

Originated by Ambassador Litho Ltd
Printed and bound in Hong Kong, China by
South China Printing Company

ISBN 0 431 18842 4
08 07 06 05 04
10 9 8 7 6 5 4 3 2 1

British Library Cataloguing in Publication Data
Gillie, Oliver
Cancer. – (Need to know)
1.Cancer – Juvenile literature
I.Title
616.9'94

Acknowledgements
The publishers would like to thank the following for permission to reproduce photographs: Alamy pp. 1 (Mark Harmel), 11 (Popperfoto), 14 (Janine Weidel Photo library), 24 (Mark Harmel), 28 (ImageState), 41 (Stock Connections), 42 (Photofusion), 46 (ImageState); Corbis pp. 21 (Tom and Dee Ann McCarthy), 23 (David Butow/SABA); Mary Evans Picture Library p. 9; PA Photos p. 51 (Owen Humphreys); Science Photo Library pp. 4 (Geoff Tompkinson), 6–7 (Dr Gopal Murti), 8 (CC Studio), 12, 13 (Will and Deni McIntyre), 15 (Josh Sher), 16, 17 (Geoff Tompkinson), 18 (Mauro Fermariello), 19 (Mauro Fermariello), 25 (Mauro Fermariello), 26 (Simon Fraser/Royal Victoria Infirmary, Newcastle), 27, 29 (Dr P Marazzi), 30 (John Cole), 33 (Colin Cuthbert), 34 (Simon Fraser/Royal Victoria Infirmary, Newcastle), 35 (Colin Cuthbert), 37 (Simon Fraser), 38 (Philippe Plailly), 43 (Chris Priest), 49 (John Cole); Matthew Zachary p. 45.

Cover photographs reproduced with permission of Corbis and SPL.

Contents

Any words appearing in the text in bold, **like this**, are explained in the Glossary.

The fight against cancer

Cancer is now the most common cause of death in developed countries. Cancer is feared because it seems to kill by stealth – appearing in otherwise healthy people and slowly reducing them to a pale shadow of their former selves. Progress in developing new treatments has been slow because there are so many different types of cancer, but thanks to medical progress, cancer can often be beaten.

"Harry Potter helped me get through some really hard and scary times. I sometimes think of Harry Potter and me as being kind of alike. He was forced into situations he could not control, and had to face an enemy he didn't know if he could beat. Harry Potter helped me to realize that with the love and support of the people around me, I could get better."

(Tyler Walton, Oaklyn, New Jersey)

Tyler's story

Cancer is rare in children, so Tyler Walton from Oaklyn, New Jersey, USA, was definitely out of luck when he became ill with **leukaemia** at the age of five. At first he seemed to be responding well to treatment. Most children are cured after two or three years, but in Tyler's case the disease returned three and a half years later, worse than ever.

The cancer invaded Tyler's bones and his spinal cord. His whole body seemed to be under attack. For months he couldn't walk and his food was given to him through a tube. It seemed as bad as it could get. His parents asked themselves if they were doing the right thing putting him through treatment which seemed worse than the disease.

Then doctors suggested a **bone marrow** transplant. Tyler's sister, Molly, was a perfect donor, because her bone marrow was a perfect match. So Tyler had a **transfusion** of Molly's bone marrow cells. After he had recovered, Tyler could once more do all the things other children could do like running, playing and eating.

During the last part of his illness Tyler's parents read aloud to him *Harry Potter and the Philosopher's Stone*. His mother Maureen got into bed with him and snuggled close while Tyler closed his eyes and listened. It was a special time for them when they escaped from drips and needles into a world of magic and adventure.

Left: A young cancer patient in hospital.

What is cancer?

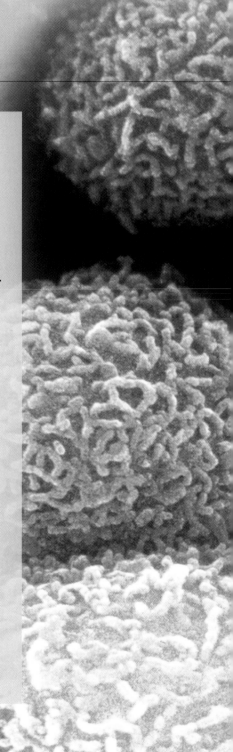

Normal body cells divide and multiply a certain number of times, and then stop because they are controlled by **hormones** and other body chemicals. After working for some months or years, normal body cells are replaced by fresh young cells which do the same job.

Cancer is the name given to disease caused by abnormal cells multiplying out of control in the body. Cancer cells behave in a different way from normal cells as a result of **mutations** in the cells.

Cancer cells generally form a small lump of tissue, a **tumour**, which becomes larger and larger. As a tumour grows, cancer cells may spread to other parts of the body. When they settle in a new area the cells continue to multiply and may form another tumour. In this way the cancer invades several parts of the body. A growing tumour may press against various body parts, such as nerves and blood vessels, or it may eat into them causing serious damage and, if it is not stopped, death.

There are more than 200 different types of cancer affecting various different parts of the body. The most common forms of cancer in adults are lung cancer, **prostate** cancer, bowel cancer and breast cancer. **Leukaemia** is a form of cancer affecting **white blood cells**, which are made in the **bone marrow**.

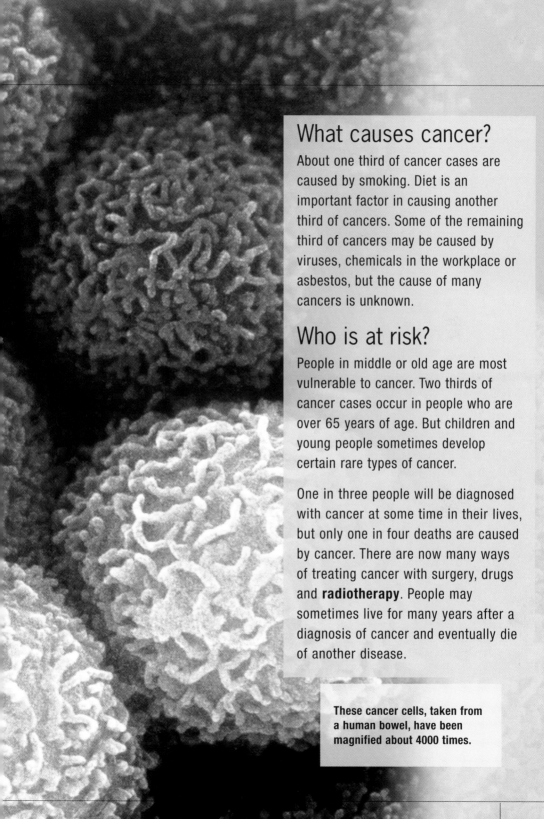

What causes cancer?

About one third of cancer cases are caused by smoking. Diet is an important factor in causing another third of cancers. Some of the remaining third of cancers may be caused by viruses, chemicals in the workplace or asbestos, but the cause of many cancers is unknown.

Who is at risk?

People in middle or old age are most vulnerable to cancer. Two thirds of cancer cases occur in people who are over 65 years of age. But children and young people sometimes develop certain rare types of cancer.

One in three people will be diagnosed with cancer at some time in their lives, but only one in four deaths are caused by cancer. There are now many ways of treating cancer with surgery, drugs and **radiotherapy**. People may sometimes live for many years after a diagnosis of cancer and eventually die of another disease.

These cancer cells, taken from a human bowel, have been magnified about 4000 times.

Cancer throughout history

Ancient records

Cancer is as old as civilization. Ancient Egyptian records describe eight cases of cancer of the breast in about 1600 BC. These **tumours** were treated with what the ancient Egyptians called 'the fire drill' – a red hot poker used to cauterize, or seal, a bleeding wound.

The Greek physician, Hippocrates, known as the 'father of medicine', used the words 'carcinos' and 'carcinoma' to describe tumours. These words come from the Greek for crab, and probably refer to leg-like projections that seem to spread from a tumour, suggesting the shape of a crab.

Microscopes developed in the 19th century enabled doctors to see cancer cells for the first time.

Scientific investigations

The first scientific investigations of cancer were undertaken by the physician Giovanni Morgagni in Padua, Italy, in 1761. He dissected the bodies of people who had died of cancer and was able to relate their illness to the position and nature of the tumour. The first doctor to take a modern approach to cancer was the Scottish surgeon John Hunter (1728–1793). He suggested how surgeons should decide whether or not to operate. He advised that a tumour could be removed if it was moveable and could be separated from surrounding tissues.

Microscopes

With the development of the modern microscope in the 19th century, doctors were for the first time able to study tumours in detail. In 1838 the German pathologist Johannes Muller showed that cancers are composed of cells like other body tissues. Another German, Rudolf Virchow (1821–1902), sometimes called the founder of **cellular pathology**, pioneered the identification of different types of cancer using the microscope. This was the foundation of modern diagnosis.

Surgery

Cancer surgery could not develop far until there were reliable methods of providing **anaesthesia** and of preventing infection. In 1865 Joseph Lister began the use of sterile instruments and other techniques for avoiding infections following surgery. About the same time simple methods of anaesthesia were developed. Slowly improvements in cancer surgery began to follow.

Chemotherapy

Drug treatment of cancer, or **chemotherapy**, began in the 1940s. As part of the US military programme, Alfred Gilman and Louis Goodman working at Yale University injected a solution of mustard gas (used as a weapon in World War I) into a mouse with cancer. The cancer disappeared and the first experiments with drugs on human cancer began shortly afterwards.

Radiotherapy

X-rays were discovered in 1895 by Wilhelm Röntgen, a Dutchman living in Germany. Radium, the radioactive material used in certain treatments, was discovered in 1898 by Madame Marie Curie, a Polish woman working in Paris. The first attempts at **radiotherapy** were made a few years later and by 1922 radiation was established as a method of treating cancer.

Rudolf Virchow identified malignant (cancerous) cells and began the scientific diagnosis of cancer.

Cancer throughout history

Tar and smoke

Prior to the 19th century, small boys as young as five years old were used to clean chimneys. The boys were bribed or beaten into climbing inside small flues, inaccessible to adults, and sweeping out the black soot. In 1775, Sir Percival Potts, a surgeon at St Bartholomew's Hospital in London, described a cancer which was found on the scrotums of boys and men who worked as sweeps. The cancer was diagnosed as a type of **sexually transmitted disease**, but Potts said this was mistaken.

Chimney sweeps in other countries, such as Germany, did not so frequently suffer from cancer of the scrotum. The Germans apparently wore better protective clothing and washed more thoroughly after work. It took another hundred years for doctors to realize that the chimney sweeps' scrotal cancer was not only caused by soot but also by tar, paraffin and other mineral oils.

In 1915 scientists at Tokyo University, Japan, put coal tar on the skin of rabbits. The rabbits developed cancer as a result. Gradually it came to be realized that all kinds of tar-containing substances can alter **genetic material** and cause normal cells to develop into cancer cells. These observations and others eventually led in 1950 to the connection being made between smoking and lung cancer. Cigarette smoke consists of a fine mist of yellow tar which is deposited in the lungs and mouth where it may change normal cells into cancer cells.

Viruses

Other causes of cancer have been known for a long time. In 1911 a virus which caused cancer in chickens was recognized by Peyton Rous working at the Rockefeller Institute in New York. Since then a number of viruses infecting people have been linked with cancer. Cancers of the female genital area and of the penis are thought to be caused by a human virus called papilloma. HIV, the virus that causes AIDS, is associated with an increased risk of developing two cancers called **Kaposi's sarcoma** and **non-Hodgkin's lymphoma**.

The dangers of tobacco smoke were not understood until after 1950. Prior to this, many people, such as British prime minister, Stanley Baldwin (shown here in the 1930s), did not realize the health risks associated with smoking.

How cancer grows and spreads

Cancer occurs when the hereditary material (**DNA**) of normal body cells changes, allowing the cells to continue to divide without control. Unlike normal cells, cancer cells continue to multiply and reproduce themselves indefinitely, so they outlive normal cells. Eventually the cancer cells form a **tumour** which consists of billions of abnormal cells.

Cancer cells do not stick together like normal cells, so individual cancer cells or small clumps of them easily drift away from the tumour. Cancer cells move round the body in the blood or in the **lymph**, the clear fluid that circulates round the body in the **lymph ducts**. Tumour cells tend to travel from the original, or primary, tumour to the nearest **lymph glands** – so this is the first place doctors generally look for signs of spread.

Secondary tumours

Cancer may spread locally in the immediate area around the primary tumour. Growths may push out from the primary tumour or small groups of cells may 'metastasize' – that is break off from the primary tumour and form what is called a secondary tumour, secondary growth or metastasis. Cancer may, for example, spread from the ovary which lies at the back of the abdomen (body cavity) to other parts of the abdomen. Lung cancer may spread to the pleura, the lining of the chest. Often the tumour cells also spread to other places, forming secondary tumours in places such as the liver, lungs, bones or brain.

Cancer cells multiply to form lumps like this breast cancer tumour (centre), made up of many abnormal cells.

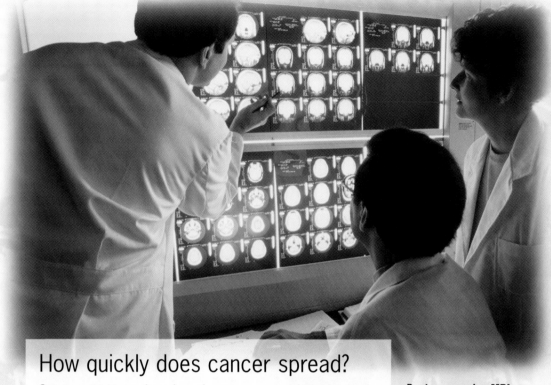

How quickly does cancer spread?

Some cancers, such as bowel cancer, grow relatively slowly and do not spread quickly. So there is a good chance that bowel cancer will not have spread if it is spotted early. If it has not spread the tumour can be removed by surgery and the patient will be completely cured. Other cancers such as lung cancer grow relatively rapidly and are not so often caught at an early stage when a complete cure is possible.

A tumour often does not cause a person any problems until it has a reached a size that can be easily seen and even then it may not cause immediate problems. Eventually a tumour becomes so large that it interferes with the working of some part of the body, for example by blocking or partially blocking the bowel. By that time the cancer has usually been growing in the body for several years.

Doctors examine **MRI scans**. These detailed images allow doctors to pinpoint the position of a tumour accurately.

Signs and symptoms of cancer

Often the first sign of cancer is not a visible lump, but a symptom that might easily be blamed on something else. A hoarse voice or headache usually go away after a few days, but when they do not go away and show no signs of improving within a few days a doctor should be consulted because they could be the first sign of something more serious. Sometimes they may be the first sign of cancer. Bowel pain, blood in the faeces or unexplained weight loss may alert doctors to bowel cancer. Lung cancer may only be detected when blood is found in the **sputum**, or when a person is investigated for a chest infection or unexplained weight loss.

The first sign of breast cancer is most often a small lump that may be felt with the fingers or only detected in an X-ray picture. The vast majority of lumps in the body are not cancer, but a new lump that does not go away after several days should always be examined by a doctor. Lumps may have many causes. For example, a lump may be caused by a harmless fluid-filled sac or **cyst**, or by a small gland that is temporarily swollen as a result of infection.

A doctor can advise about persistent problems that might be a sign of cancer.

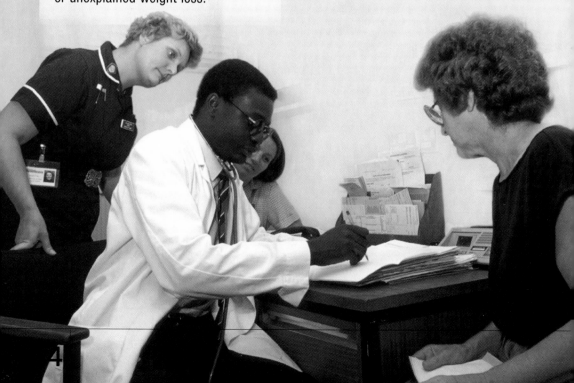

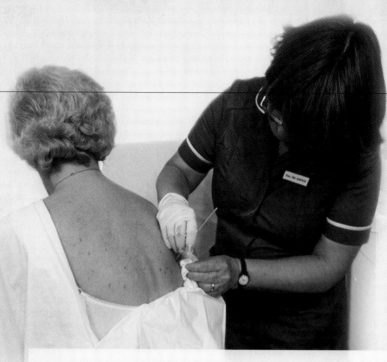

A nurse removes a mole from a woman's back. Once it has been removed, tests will be able to show whether or not it is malignant.

Warning signs of cancer

If a person develops one or more of the signs below, it does not necessarily mean the person has cancer. But if the symptoms persist a doctor should be consulted.

Type of cancer	Warning signs
Bowel	persistent diarrhoea/constipation or a combination of the two; blood in the faeces; unexplained weight loss
Brain	headaches (but many people get these and they don't have cancer); weakness in limbs; slurred speech; personality changes
Breast	painless lump; bleeding or discharge from a nipple; change in breast size or shape
Leukaemia	tiredness; lots of infections; increased bruising; bleeding gums
Lung	persistent cough; chest/shoulder pain; difficulty in breathing; hoarse voice; blood in the sputum; unexplained weight loss; repeated chest infection
Prostate	delay in flow when passing urine; reduced speed of urine flow; dribbling urine; pain on passing urine; blood in urine
Skin	a mole that enlarges, bleeds, itches, changes appearance, or becomes an irregular shape; colour is important: moles should normally be one colour, more than two colours in a mole is suspicious; sores that don't heal after three weeks

Diagnosis of cancer

People usually see a doctor if they have a symptom such as a persistent hoarse voice or discomfort in the bowel and change of bowel habit. A series of tests must then be carried out before the doctor is able to say what the cause of the problem is.

There are three main types of test for all cancers: imaging, cytology and chemical tests.

Imaging

Images of the inside parts of the body obtained by X-rays are one of the commonest ways of diagnosing cancer. Better X-ray pictures can be obtained of the bowel, for example, if a person swallows barium (a barium meal). The barium reflects the X-rays and so makes the bowel show up very clearly. X-ray examination of the breast, known as **mammography**, enables lumps to be found that are too small to feel.

X-rays or other methods can also be used to produce cross-sectional pictures built up by computer. These **CT**, **MRI** and **PET** scans enable very accurate location of a **tumour**. Images may also be obtained by use of **ultrasound** and by use of radioactive substances (radionuclides).

Cytology

Cytology is the study of cells under the microscope. A small sample, or **biopsy**, is taken from the suspect tissue and specially prepared for examination under the microscope. The sample may be taken with a needle or, in the case of the cervix (the neck of the womb), a sample of cells may be gently scraped off using a plastic scraper. Looking at the cells under the microscope, a specialist can see whether or not the cells are **malignant**.

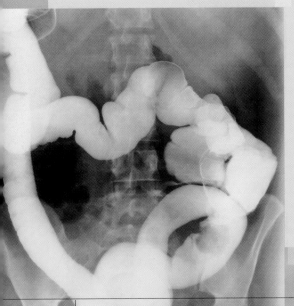

A barium meal is given to a patient before an X-ray of the bowel is taken. The barium shows up the bowel and the tumour (lower right of the picture).

Chemical tests

Chemical tests involve taking a sample of urine, faeces, blood, or other body tissue in a small tube and testing for the presence of certain chemicals. The presence of a chemical may suggest to the doctor that cancer is a possibility. Chemical tests may be used to see if there is a problem that cannot easily be detected in other ways. Faeces may, for example, be examined for hidden blood. If hidden blood is present there must be bleeding into the bowel, which could be caused by a tumour.

❝I find myself more comfortable telling people: 'I was diagnosed with cancer' instead of saying: 'I have cancer'. On some deep level I do not want to own this illness.❞

(Breast cancer survivor)

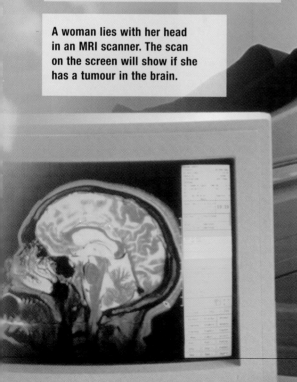

A woman lies with her head in an MRI scanner. The scan on the screen will show if she has a tumour in the brain.

Screening tests

Cancer can be treated most effectively when it is detected and identified before it has spread to other parts of the body. This may be done with **screening tests**. These tests can pick up cancer when a person is still feeling completely well, years before the cancer might begin to make them ill. If a cancer can be detected at an early stage the chance of treatment being effective is greater and the patient is more likely to make a full recovery.

The simplest form of screening is self-examination. Young men should examine their testes regularly and seek medical advice if an unusual lump is found.

If it is detected early, testicular cancer can be treated more simply and effectively. If women examine their breasts regularly, an unusual lump may be detected early and a full medical examination may then be obtained. Screening for breast cancer by taking an X-ray (**mammography**) also enables the disease to be caught at an early stage and so simpler treatment can be given. Breast screening programmes are generally limited to women over 45 or 50, who are at higher risk of developing breast cancer than younger women.

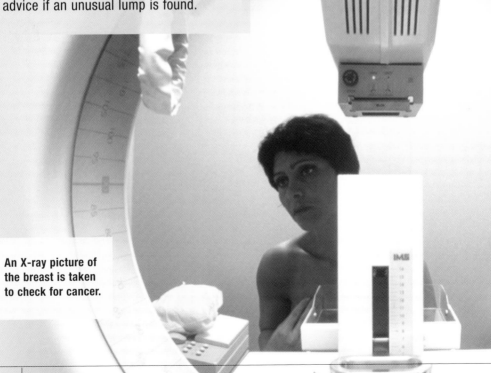

An X-ray picture of the breast is taken to check for cancer.

Screening for cancer of the cervix (neck of the womb) has reduced the number of deaths from cervical cancer by about half. Screening tests are carried out by taking a scraping of cells from the neck of the womb and examining them under a microscope. In this way the disease can be picked up at an early stage and cured by surgical removal of the **malignant** cells.

As many as 3 people in 1000 over the age of 60 have been found to have bowel cancer when examined by sigmoidoscope – this is a long flexible tube which can be used to examine the lower bowel. But the procedure is expensive and it is only practical to use it when some other sign such as blood in the faeces suggests a problem. Early detection greatly improves the chance of a person surviving bowel cancer.

Prostate cancer may also be detected using a blood test for 'prostate specific antigen' (PSA). However, use of this screening test is controversial because many doctors believe the test is not accurate enough. Some doctors are enthusiastic about screening for prostate cancer arguing that it saves lives. Others argue against using the PSA test because it is not completely reliable.

No screening programme is 100 per cent accurate. Some people who have cancer will be missed and they may then have a false sense of security. Other people who do not have the disease are sometimes falsely recorded as having it. These people suffer unnecessary treatment and needless anxiety.

A technician examines cells taken from the cervix (neck of the womb). Cancer cells have an unusual appearance.

Food and cancer

Experts broadly agree that about a third of cancer deaths are caused primarily by the food we eat. There are a few foods, such as certain types of salted fish eaten in China, or peanuts contaminated by growth of fungus, that have been shown to cause cancer when consumed regularly over long periods. However, in most cases the risk of cancer seems to be increased not by eating one particular food but rather by the combination of ingredients in the diet as a whole. The risk of cancer can be reduced by diets that are low in fat and high in fibre, high in vegetables and fruits, and high in grain products such as bread, cereals and pasta.

Fat

Cancer of the breast, bowel, and **prostate** have been linked to diets that are high in fat and oil which comes mostly from spreads, cooking fats, and fat in meat and dairy products. Countries which have a high consumption of fat have a higher proportion of these cancers in the population. The type of fat does not seem to be as important as the total quantity of fat that is eaten.

Alcohol

Taking more than three alcoholic drinks per day is linked to an increase in the risk of developing cancer, particularly cancer of the mouth, throat and oesophagus. Taking more than six drinks per day is associated with a 60 per cent increase in the average risk of cancer.

Obesity

People who are obese (seriously overweight) have an increased risk of certain cancers including those of the breast, womb, bowel, kidney, oesophagus, stomach and gallbladder.

Vegetables and fruits

Diets that are low in vegetables and fruits are believed to increase the risk of certain forms of cancer, including cancer of the lung, bowel, breast, mouth, stomach, and ovaries. Vegetables and fruits contain substances that protect against cancer, including fibre, vitamins A and C, and carotenoids (the yellow and red coloured substances found particularly in carrots, melons, and dark green vegetables). This has led to campaigns for people to eat five servings of vegetables and fruits per day – a serving is one average sized apple, pear, orange, or banana or two small fruits such as kiwis or plums, or an equivalent amount of vegetable.

Fibre

Fibre is the part of food that is not digested in the human body. Fibre is found in grain products as well as vegetables and fruits. A high consumption of whole grains, taken as wholemeal/wholegrain bread or breakfast cereal, appears to protect against cancer of the bowel.

Cancer and smoking

Smoking causes the deaths of hundreds of thousands of people every year all over the world. They die not just of various types of cancer but also of heart disease and strokes. One third of all cancers are caused by smoking.

Lung cancer accounts for more than a quarter of all deaths from cancer and most lung cancer is caused by smoking. Cigarette smoke can cause cancer of all the parts of the body it comes into contact with apart from the fingers. It causes cancer of the larynx (voice box), the inside of the mouth, the tongue, the lips, and the oesophagus (the tube taking food to the stomach).

The risk of developing cancer depends on how much a person smokes – the more a person smokes the greater their chance of developing cancer. The younger a person is when they start to smoke the greater the risk of developing cancer. People who give up smoking greatly reduce their risk of dying of cancer caused by tobacco.

It is now recognized that 'passive smoking' (breathing in tobacco smoke in the air) is a significant cause of lung cancer in non-smokers. A person who works next to a smoker or lives in a house where people smoke may have their risk of developing lung cancer increased by between 30 and 50 per cent.

Treatment of lung cancer

Current treatment of lung cancer is not very effective, although some advances are being made. There are several different types of lung cancer and a patient's future depends on the type and the stage of the cancer. Surgery is possible in some patients with lung cancer and these patients probably have the best chance of long-term survival. **Radiotherapy** and **chemotherapy** are the more usual forms of treatment. These produce good short-term results over a period of six months to two years and long-term survival is possible.

Suffering the consequences

Deborah Norton began smoking at the age of 12 and at 47 discovered she had cancer of the larynx. A month later she had her larynx completely removed and now breathes through a tube in her neck. She says 'No one wants to live like this out of choice. But, it was a choice I made without realizing the consequences. If I can help just one person to stop smoking, I will continue to speak out.'

❝[Smoking is] the chief single, avoidable cause of death in our society and the most important public health issue of our time.❞

(C. Everett Koop, former surgeon general of the USA)

Breast cancer

Breast cancer is most often detected as a small lump in the breast. Frequently it is found by the woman herself but it may be picked up on an X-ray during **screening** (**mammography**). Breast cancer is the most common form of cancer in women other than skin cancer. It is a devastating diagnosis for a woman – but better treatment and earlier detection has lead to an improvement in the survival rate of women with breast cancer over the last 20 years.

The pink ribbon is the symbol worn by people who support breast cancer awareness and research.

What causes breast cancer?

It is not known exactly what causes breast cancer but certain conditions and lifestyles have been found to increase the risk of breast cancer. For example, women have an increased risk of breast cancer if they drink between two and five alcoholic drinks a day, if they are overweight, or if they put on a lot of weight as an adult. The risk of breast cancer is also greater for women who have close relatives who had the disease before the age of 50.

Treatment

Operations to treat breast cancer aim to remove the **tumour** in the breast to prevent further spread of the cancer. The type of operation advised will depend on how advanced the cancer is. If the tumour is at an early stage, a removal of the lump with a small amount of surrounding tissue (called a lumpectomy) is carried out. However, if the cancer has begun to spread from the breast then a radical

mastectomy is likely to be carried out. This involves the removal of the entire breast as well as some of the **lymph glands** in the armpit.

Operations are generally followed by **radiotherapy**, **chemotherapy** and/or **hormone therapy** to kill any remaining cancer cells in the area of the breast. The hormone drug Tamoxifen is generally given for about five years after surgery to help prevent the cancer from returning.

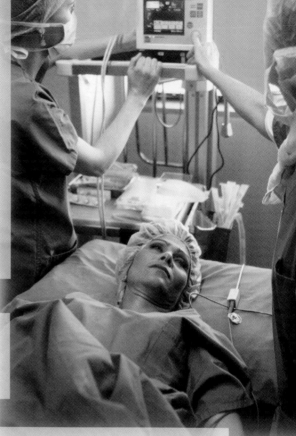

Doctors monitor a woman who is recovering from an operation to remove a tumour from the breast.

Non-cancerous lumps

Ideally a woman should examine her breasts every month to look for any change. If a change is detected or there is a discharge or blood coming from the nipple she should consult a doctor. Eight out of ten breast lumps are not cancer. They may be the result of fibrocystic disease. In this disease one or both breasts become lumpy and tender in the week or so before a period begins. The lumps are caused by harmless fluid-filled sacs. Lumps in the breast may also form because of fibroadenoma. These are harmless rubbery growths that can be moved about under the skin and cause no pain.

Leukaemia

Leukaemia is the most common cancer in children but it also occurs in adults. It is a cancer of the **white blood cells**, which are made in the **bone marrow** in the centre of bones. White blood cells are important for defending the body against infections. But people with leukaemia have abnormally large numbers of white cells in their blood. There may be so many of them that they do not leave sufficient space for the red blood cells which are necessary to carry oxygen from the lungs round the body. They also do not leave space in the bone marrow for other normal cells.

Types of leukaemia

There are many different types of leukaemia. They are named according to the cells they are derived from in the bone marrow, the lymphocytes or the myelocytes, and according to whether the leukaemia is **chronic** or **acute**. In acute leukaemia the white blood cells divide rapidly but do not mature properly. In chronic leukaemia the cells look normal but live longer than normal and so build up in the blood.

This boy with leukaemia has lost all his hair following drug treatment to kill cancer cells.

White blood cells (the light-coloured cells) from a person with leukaemia have become malignant (cancerous) and multiplied, leaving little space for normal red blood cells (dark pink).

What causes leukaemia?

Leukaemia is sometimes caused by exposure to radiation or chemicals that damage **DNA**, the hereditary material of the cell. It is a risk, for example, for workers in atomic power stations. For this reason they are strictly regulated so that they do not spend too long exposed to radiation. However, the damage to DNA most often happens by accident during periods of rapid cell growth when the DNA is being copied very frequently. The more cells multiply the greater the chance of an error occurring in the copying of DNA.

Treatment of leukaemia

Treatment of leukaemia in children is generally very successful. About 75 per cent of children now survive five or more years after the illness began.

Treatment varies according to the type of leukaemia. At first, drugs (**chemotherapy**) are given to kill as many of the cancer cells as possible and induce a **remission** – that is a temporary reduction in the severity of the disease when the number of cancer cells has been greatly reduced. After a short rest to give the patient time to recover, more drugs are given to rid the body of the last few cancer cells. This may be followed by **radiotherapy** to kill cancer cells that remain in the bone marrow. This treatment is sufficient to cure many patients. If the disease returns again, a bone marrow transplant may be possible if a suitable donor can be found.

Skin cancer

Skin cancer is the most common form of cancer. There are two major types: **melanoma**, which accounts for only about 4 per cent of skin cancer cases but 80 per cent of skin cancer deaths, and **non-melanoma skin cancer**. Any new growth on the skin, a spot or lump that is getting larger, or a sore that does not heal in three months, might be skin cancer and should be examined by a doctor.

Melanoma

Melanoma is generally first noticed as a dark coloured spot on the skin resembling a mole. A normal mole is an evenly coloured brown, black or tan spot on the skin which may be flat or raised up and may be round or oval. Normal moles generally stay the same size for many years. Melanoma forms a much more irregular spot. Occasionally a normal mole may develop into melanoma.

Non-melanoma skin cancer

Non-melanoma skin cancers are generally spotted early and are easily treated. They usually appear on parts of the body such as the head and neck, lips and the back of the hands that are most frequently exposed to the sun. They grow relatively slowly and rarely spread far.

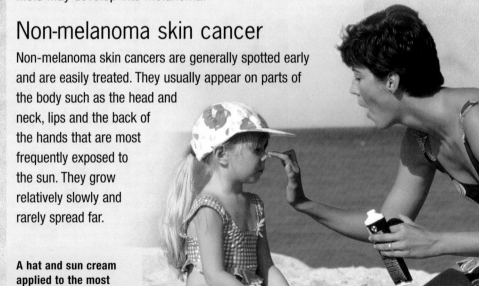

A hat and sun cream applied to the most exposed parts protects against burning and skin cancer.

Safety in the sun

Extensive exposure to strong sunlight, particularly when it leads to sunburn, increases the risk of skin cancer. People who work outdoors and have fair skin are most at risk. They need to wear suitable clothing and a hat to protect themselves from sunburn. They should also use sunscreen (with protection factor of 15 or more), although this is not as effective as clothing and a hat.

While care must be taken to avoid sunburn, it is important not to avoid sunlight completely. Exposure of the skin to sunlight for about ten minutes per day is desirable to ensure a good supply of vitamin D, which is now believed to protect against certain cancers including melanoma.

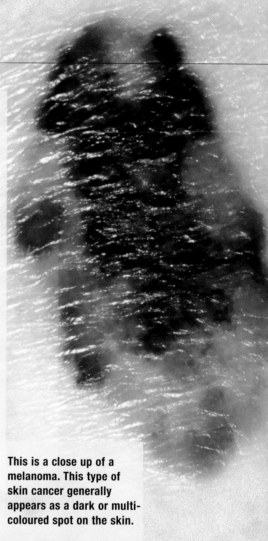

This is a close up of a melanoma. This type of skin cancer generally appears as a dark or multi-coloured spot on the skin.

Warning signs of melanoma

It is important to examine moles on the skin and look for any changes. If any of the following are observed, a doctor should be consulted to check whether the mole is normal:

- One half of the mole does not match the other half
- The edges of the mole are ragged or notched
- The colour of the mole is not the same all over
- The mole is wider than about 6 mm
- Any change in size or appearance of the mole.

Cancer in children

Children rarely get cancer and when they do they can often be cured. Nevertheless cancer is the most common cause of death other than accidents in children under fourteen years of age.

The most common form of cancer in children is **leukaemia**, which accounts for about one third of all cancer cases in children. After that brain **tumours**, which are relatively rare in adults, are the most common childhood cancer.

Some childhood cancers begin in the first few months of life while the baby is still in the womb, although they may not be noticed until the child is several years old. These 'embryonal cancers' arise from cells that have failed to develop in the normal way and eventually become **malignant**. Examples of such embryonal cancers are retinoblastoma, which occurs in the eye, and hepatoblastoma, which occurs in the liver.

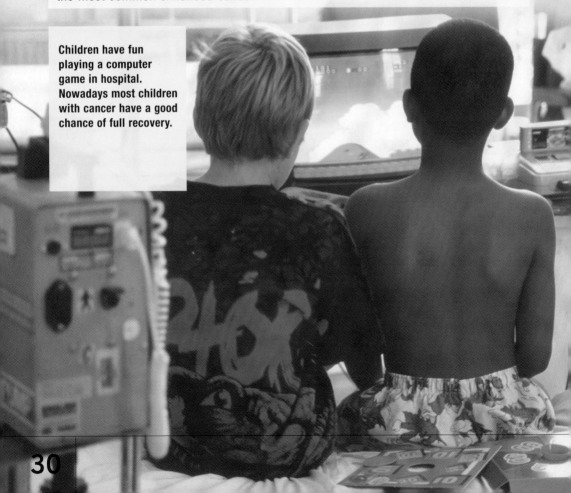

Children have fun playing a computer game in hospital. Nowadays most children with cancer have a good chance of full recovery.

Treatment of childhood cancer

Cancers that affect children tend to be sensitive to drugs and so very good results are obtained in treating cancer in children. In the 1960s, before the introduction of modern **chemotherapy**, children with cancer could not be treated effectively and most of them died. Today the drugs used in chemotherapy are combined together in various ways and much better results are obtained, with about 70 per cent of children who have had cancer surviving into adulthood.

Chemotherapy rapidly produces **remission** of the disease but the treatment needs to be repeated several times and may be combined with surgery or **radiotherapy** to ensure that all malignant cells in the body are destroyed. Treatment can last more than a year and success varies with the type of cancer.

Treatment must be undertaken in highly specialized centres, where doctors and nurses have accumulated experience of the best way to use these powerful drugs and staff know how to help the children through a very difficult time.

Cancer is not an infectious disease

Occasionally two children in the same school, or the same area, or very occasionally in the same family develop cancer. When these cases have been investigated they have generally been found to occur together by chance. Parents often feel guilty and try to think of things they did which might have caused a child to develop cancer. The cause of childhood cancers is not known and so parents should not blame themselves.

Treating cancer

Surgery

Surgery is often the best way to remove a **tumour** and, if cancer cells have not spread, surgery is likely to result in a complete cure. However surgery may not be possible if the tumour is large or awkwardly placed or if the cancer has spread locally to involve a large area of tissue.

In order to have the best chance of removing every bit of the cancer, the surgeon will generally remove a wide band of tissue from around the tumour, or remove the whole of the affected organ together with the tumour. The surgeon will generally remove local **lymph glands** and **lymph ducts** near the tumour. This is because the lymph glands are generally the first place that small groups of cells breaking away from the main tumour will settle. There are many lymph glands in the body so the removal of a few does not have a serious effect on the body's defence against infection.

Surgery is often followed by treatment with **radiotherapy** or drugs (**chemotherapy**). This is done in order to kill any cancer cells that have spread to other parts of the body and have not been removed by the surgeon. Sometimes these therapies are given before surgery in order to shrink the tumour and induce **remission**, making surgery easier.

Pain-killing drugs are given after the operation to make the patient more comfortable and to enable the patient to move about more easily. It is important for patients to move about as soon as possible after surgery in order to prevent chest infections and dangerous blood clots.

Skating to recovery

Molly McMaster was told she had cancer on her 23rd birthday. She was an ice-skating teacher and hockey coach and dreamt of playing one day for the US women's hockey team. But she became unwell and was forced to return home to Glen Falls, New York. She had emergency surgery and 60 cm of her colon (bowel) were removed together with a large tumour. 'I was in really good physical shape when I went into this and I think that it helped,' said Molly. Following the surgery and chemotherapy treatment, Molly skated from Glen Falls to Greeley, Colorado, on a 71-day 2000-mile trip to raise money for cancer research.

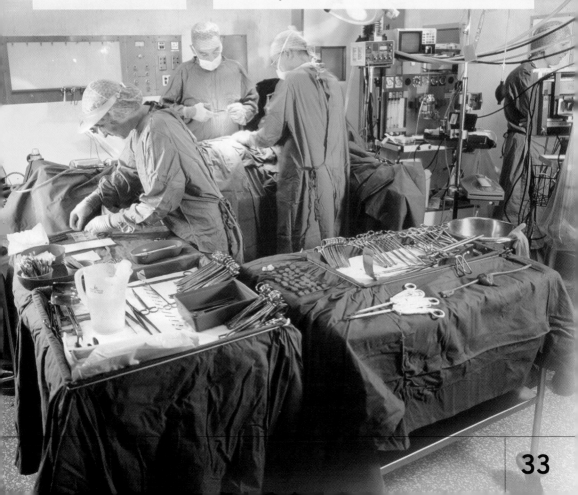

Surgeons remove a prostate gland that contains a tumour. Prostate cancer is a common cancer in older men.

Treating cancer

Chemotherapy

Chemotherapy is the medical name given to the treatment of cancer with drugs. Chemotherapy may cure a cancer or it may be used to reduce the size of the cancer and induce remission. A complete course of chemotherapy usually takes several months. It may be given before or after surgery or radiotherapy, or it may be given by itself.

The drugs used in chemotherapy are only able to kill cancer cells when they are dividing, so cancer cells that are not dividing at the time of treatment will survive. By the time the next treatment starts some of these 'resting' cells will have started to divide and they will then be killed. Normal body cells that are dividing at the time of treatment are killed in the same way as the cancer cells. However, there are many more normal body cells than cancer cells, and normal body cells are generally more robust. So the cancer cells are eliminated while most of the body cells survive.

Side effects

It is normal to feel extremely tired during chemotherapy because the drugs cause a lot of damage to body cells and tissues which must be repaired. The body is also short of **white blood cells** because they divide frequently and so many are killed during chemotherapy. This means that the body is less resistant to infection.

A doctor discusses treatment with a patient who has leukaemia. Treatment may take months and needs to be planned to allow for rest periods.

The hair and the skin are growing all the time. Cells lining the digestive system are constantly replacing themselves and cells in the **bone marrow** are also growing very actively to replace blood cells. As chemotherapy kills normal cells that are dividing, these are the parts of the body that are most severely affected by chemotherapy. The main side effects are fatigue, nausea, vomiting, a sore mouth, increased risk of infection and loss of hair. These side effects will stop once the treatment comes to an end and the hair will then re-grow.

Some cancer drugs cause infertility, which may be temporary or permanent. Before treatment begins, men may put some of their sperm into a sperm bank, where it can be stored for later use, and women may sometimes put their eggs or tissue from their ovaries into storage. They may then be able to have children at a later date when they are ready to have a family.

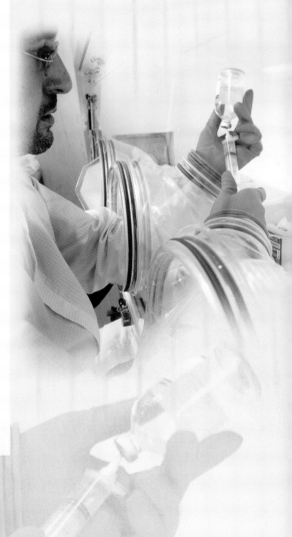

A hospital pharmacist prepares a cancer drug in a special cabinet designed to make sure the drug is not contaminated.

Radiotherapy

Radiotherapy, uses a beam of radiation, usually X-rays, to destroy cancer cells. The beam is focused on a tumour or area of tissue so that the energy is concentrated in one place. Radiotherapy beams use a much higher quantity of energy than is used when an X-ray picture is taken. Treatment is often repeated over a period of several weeks.

The radiation damages the **DNA** of the cancer cells and so makes it impossible for them to continue to grow. Normal cells are also damaged but there are more of them and they are generally better able to repair themselves. Healthy body tissue can be shielded from the effects of radiation with a special apron containing sheets of lead.

Radiotherapy is particularly useful in the treatment of cancer in areas such as the tongue, the throat or the brain which have a complicated structure that may make them unsuitable for surgery. Radiation is also a convenient way of treating cancer of the skin, the breast or the cervix because other tissues or organs are not in the way and side effects are therefore minimal.

Radiation treatment may also be delivered to a small area by means of a **radioactive implant**. In this method, the implant – a small pellet or a wire of radioactive material (radium, uranium or cobalt 60) – is placed into the tumour and left there for a few days. **Gamma rays** emitted by the implant destroy the surrounding tissue. This method is often used to treat cancer of the tongue, the womb and the cervix.

Radiotherapy may also be given by mouth as a medicine. Radioactive iodine may be given, for example, to treat cancer of the **thyroid gland**. First, as much as possible of the gland is removed by surgery. Then radioactive iodine is given as a drink. Any remaining cells from the thyroid gland pick up the iodine. The iodine then releases radiation, destroying the remaining thyroid cells, with minimal damage to nearby tissues. Normal cells do not concentrate the iodine and so remain unchanged.

Side effects

Radiotherapy treatments are painless in themselves but they do have side effects. Tiredness is the most common side effect. Frequently radiotherapy causes skin irritation and a temporary change of skin colour in the area affected by the radiation beam. Hair may also be lost when the beam of radiation crosses the scalp but will grow back again. Radiotherapy may have to be repeated after a rest period to ensure that all cancer cells are killed.

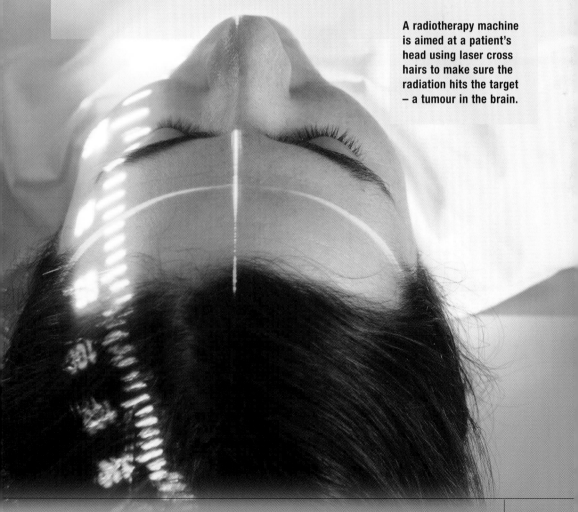

A radiotherapy machine is aimed at a patient's head using laser cross hairs to make sure the radiation hits the target – a tumour in the brain.

Transplants

A new generation of cancer treatments has been developed in the last decade. These methods have not in any way replaced the tried and tested methods of surgery, radiotherapy and chemotherapy but they have enabled some cancers to be treated that could not be treated before. Surgeons are now able to remove organs from one person, the donor, and transplant them into another person – for example when a person's kidneys have stopped working. Transplants of bone marrow or blood cells are being used as part of the treatment of certain types of cancer.

Bone marrow transplants may be used to treat **leukaemia**. Bone marrow contains **stem cells** which constantly divide to give rise to white blood cells, which defend the body against infection. The stem cells may become **malignant** and then give rise to leukaemic cells. Conventional radiotherapy and chemotherapy treatments are used to kill the malignant stem cells and this is sufficient to cure many people who have leukaemia. If this treatment fails a transplant may be possible.

When a transplant has been arranged, heavier doses of chemotherapy can be given to kill the malignant stem cells that remain. But all the normal stem cells are killed at the same time. So a donor, with carefully matched cells, must be available who can provide normal bone marrow cells to be transplanted into the patient. The donor marrow is given to the patient in the same way as a blood **transfusion**.

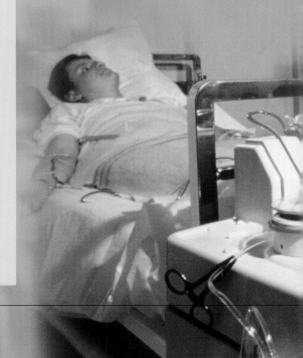

A patient is being prepared for a transplant. Stem cells are collected which will be returned to the patient following high-dose chemotherapy.

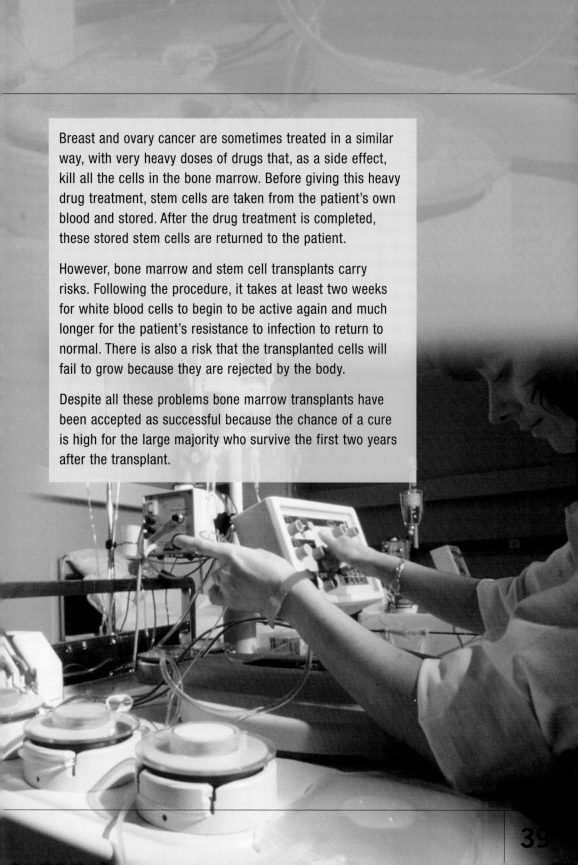

Breast and ovary cancer are sometimes treated in a similar way, with very heavy doses of drugs that, as a side effect, kill all the cells in the bone marrow. Before giving this heavy drug treatment, stem cells are taken from the patient's own blood and stored. After the drug treatment is completed, these stored stem cells are returned to the patient.

However, bone marrow and stem cell transplants carry risks. Following the procedure, it takes at least two weeks for white blood cells to begin to be active again and much longer for the patient's resistance to infection to return to normal. There is also a risk that the transplanted cells will fail to grow because they are rejected by the body.

Despite all these problems bone marrow transplants have been accepted as successful because the chance of a cure is high for the large majority who survive the first two years after the transplant.

Treating cancer

Alex's story

Alex Harris is a financial analyst with a passion for cycle riding. But he thought his cycling days might be over when he found a painful bump on his shin and learnt it was cancer.

Now he is more determined than ever to get on his bike.

'I had a goal, and the goal was to go out to Texas and ride in the Ride for the Roses cycle race and complete it. That's kind of what got me through I guess, just being stubborn and having a goal,' said Alex who lives in Huntsville, Alabama, USA. The race was inspired by champion bike racer, Lance Armstrong, who won the Tour de France cycle race three years running after recovering from testicular cancer.

Alex's doctors told him that the standard treatment for his cancer, a rare type of **sarcoma**, was a **bone graft** and chemotherapy but they were not going to recommend them because the statistics did not show that they worked. Nevertheless they hoped to save his leg with a course of radiotherapy.

Alex had six weeks of radiotherapy and five operations. The first operation removed the tumour. But his progress was complicated by an infection of the bone and three more operations were needed.

Nothing was simple. Alex had an allergic reaction to the antibiotic drugs he was being given, and he was given some 60 treatments with hyperbaric oxygen, that is oxygen under pressure in a special chamber. But he came through them all and was finally able to compete in the Ride for the Roses.

Alex says that cancer has given him a new appreciation of life. When there is a moment of joy he grasps it, relishes it and does not let it go. There was one of those moments on a recent cycle ride.

'We were rolling through a neighbourhood and passed a house with two little girls playing in the backyard. One was bouncing on a trampoline and the other was spraying her with a hose. I can still hear the squeals of laughter,' said Alex. 'A year ago I would never have recognized how beautiful that sound is, much less remembered it.'

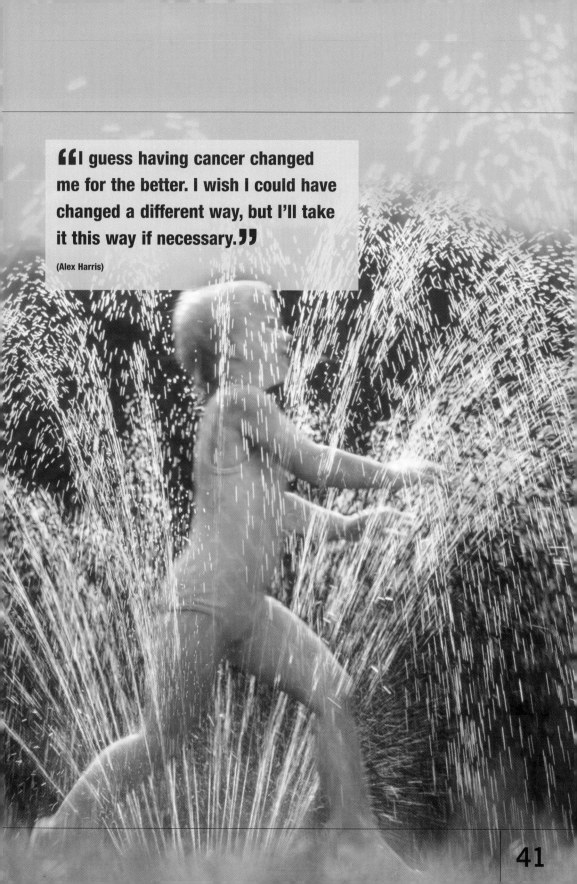

❝I guess having cancer changed me for the better. I wish I could have changed a different way, but I'll take it this way if necessary.❞

(Alex Harris)

Anxieties and fears

When a person is diagnosed as having cancer he or she will often experience anxiety which can be very severe. Anxiety may make the pain experienced by cancer sufferers feel worse. It may also disturb sleep, increase tiredness and so delay full recovery. Anxiety can also be a major factor in nausea and vomiting. Nevertheless anxiety is a normal response to stressful events and is part of the process of coming to terms with an illness.

Fear of the unknown

Fear of the unknown is often a significant cause of anxiety. Patients may feel less anxious when they are given more information about their illness and their treatment, or when they find out more from booklets available from cancer charities and patient groups or from websites. Patients also usually begin to feel less anxious as they become more accustomed to seeing doctors and going to hospitals. As they get to know hospital staff they gradually feel more at ease and less threatened by fears of the unknown.

Cancer forces young people to think about life and make difficult decisions.

Anxieties about treatment

Anxiety may also arise during the course of hospital treatment. Poorly controlled pain and severe side effects of treatment such as nausea and exhaustion may make a person anxious about a further course of treatment. In these circumstances discussion with medical staff will be of great help. Medical and nursing staff may suggest modifying the treatment schedule in some way. This gives the patient an important feeling of control, which in turn may reduce anxiety.

Relaxation

Relaxation is also important. The best way to relax varies greatly from one person to another. For one person, listening to music or playing board or card games with friends may be a good way. For others talking with friends and family about ordinary things may be best. Special tapes designed to encourage relaxation can be very effective. Massage and aromatherapy are good ways for other people.

Signs of severe anxiety

Severe anxiety can be brought on by a diagnosis of cancer, or by other life events. Signs of severe anxiety include:
- intense fears
- inability to absorb information
- inability to cooperate with medical staff
- shortness of breath
- sweating
- trembling
- light-headedness or dizziness
- sensation of rapid heartbeat (palpitations).

Much information about cancer and its treatment is available from hospitals and charities.

Recovering from brain cancer

Matthew's story

One question concerned Matthew Zachary before he had surgery for a brain **tumour**. He did not ask his doctor: 'Am I going to live?' only: 'Am I going to be able to play the piano again?'

Matthew was 21 years old and studying for a music degree at Binghamton University, New York. He had struggled with a weakness in his left hand that threatened to prevent him from playing. Doctors thought at first it was carpel tunnel syndrome, irritation to a nerve in his wrist, caused by the demands of practising piano 80 hours a week. But a few weeks later his speech became slurred and he had trouble walking.

A scan showed that Matthew had a tumour the size of a golf ball in the lower part of his brain. Two weeks later the tumour was removed surgically. When he got back home he found he could play the piano again. Without his piano playing Matthew had felt lost, now life was worthwhile once more. However, he could not play as he had done before.

The operation on his brain had affected his ability to move his fingers and he had to retrain his left hand.

After his operation doctors gave Matthew only a 60 per cent chance of living for five years. He had to return to hospital for **radiotherapy** that made him feel awful, but he worked out his feelings with jazz improvisation on the piano.

With a lot of hard work Matthew completed his degree. He was then advised to take a one-year course of **chemotherapy** in order to be sure that all the cancer cells were killed. But he asked some questions and found that the proposed drug treatment might damage nerves in his hands and could only be expected to add five months to his life.

'I would rather live to age 26 and die being able to play the piano, than live to 26 and a half and not be able to play,' he said.

Since then Matthew has rebuilt his life and so far the cancer has not returned. He now plays the piano professionally and has starred in a number of charity events to raise money for cancer research.

"Everything that happens to you, whether you like it or not, becomes a part of your life. You must live your life and be the best you can be every step of the way."

(Matthew Zachary, pictured)

Friends and family

Breaking bad news

It is not easy to tell people bad news. A person with cancer may not feel able to talk about their illness right away. It may take time for a person with cancer to absorb information about their illness and find the right words to be able to tell others. Sometimes patients want their distress to be kept private – especially at the beginning. But it may come as a relief when friends and family do know. The person with cancer can then enjoy receiving greetings and visits from friends which provide what is often a vital lifeline.

Relaxation with friends and family is an important way of overcoming the stress of cancer treatment.

Links to a normal world

For people with cancer, friends and family are an important link with the normal world outside hospital. People with cancer want to feel that they are still actively connected and involved with this world even though the hospital ward and treatment isolate them. Patients want to hear good and bad news of family and friends so they do not feel excluded.

Sharing feelings and listening

People with cancer often do not want advice. People who give advice often do not know all the circumstances, and even if they are well informed too much advice can just create additional worry. People with cancer often find it more helpful if friends and family ask questions and listen. Laughter and talking about other things will often help to make a person with cancer feel normal. Sometimes holding hands and crying together brings people closer and makes everyone feel better.

Baseball cap replaces hair

Michele Conley was told she would lose all her hair within three weeks of her first **chemotherapy**. Michele, 39, asked her children whether they would prefer her to wear a wig or a baseball cap. They voted for the baseball cap. But when her hair began to come out in fistfuls she started to wear a wig. She wasn't ready to look at herself in the mirror or let her children see her bald head. 'A very feminine part of me was gone,' said Michele. When she did show them her head her children said: 'Cool, you look like Michael Jordan.' She felt free – and after that only wore the baseball cap.

❝Being diagnosed with cancer accelerates your life. You appreciate the time you have. It's pulled my family more lovingly tight than we have ever been.❞

(Andy Cayton, cancer survivor)

Hospices and palliative care

Even when cancer cannot be cured a person may still have a period of life ahead which may be better enjoyed with the right kind of help. Palliative care, which aims to slow the cancer down and control any pain, will make it possible for a cancer patient to be more active and may provide months or even years of life.

Palliative care uses **radiotherapy** or **chemotherapy** to delay the growth of **tumours** when it is no longer possible to eradicate them entirely. However, cancer cells become resistant to radiotherapy and chemotherapy and so these treatments tend to become increasingly ineffective.

When people with cancer become very ill and do not have long to live they may enter a hospice, a home that provides specialist care for sick people who are not expected to get better. The first modern hospice was founded in 1967 by Dame Cicely Saunders in London, UK. It was based on ancient ideas of hospitality and charity. A hospice was originally a place of shelter and rest for weary and sick travellers. Now a hospice is a place where travellers at the end of life's journey may find peace.

Hospices have developed special knowledge and skill in controlling pain and in providing compassionate care. They aim to enable people to enjoy their last days or weeks of life in dignity surrounded by their family and friends. They seek to treat the person rather than the disease and neither hasten death nor postpone it. Instead, they try to make life comfortable for the patient while allowing the patient to remain in control.

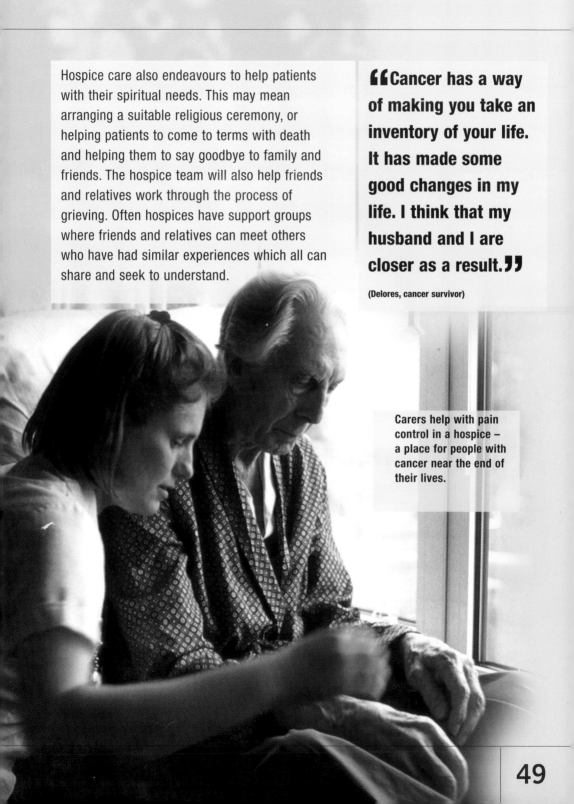

Hospice care also endeavours to help patients with their spiritual needs. This may mean arranging a suitable religious ceremony, or helping patients to come to terms with death and helping them to say goodbye to family and friends. The hospice team will also help friends and relatives work through the process of grieving. Often hospices have support groups where friends and relatives can meet others who have had similar experiences which all can share and seek to understand.

❝Cancer has a way of making you take an inventory of your life. It has made some good changes in my life. I think that my husband and I are closer as a result.❞

(Delores, cancer survivor)

Carers help with pain control in a hospice – a place for people with cancer near the end of their lives.

Hope in the fight against cancer

Researchers have made great progress in understanding cancer. New cancer cases and cancer deaths are falling overall. **Screening tests** for cancer of the breast and cancer of the cervix are bringing earlier diagnosis and treatment and are saving lives.

Hope in the fight against cancer

Scientists have found key **genes** in cancer cells that cause them to grow out of control, and are beginning to understand why this happens. Eventually they will develop new drugs that will be able to prevent the growth of cancer cells more effectively.

At present, new drugs are just beginning to become available that make use of **immune reactions** to provide new ways of treating cancer. They include **monoclonal antibodies** and other forms of immune treatment such as cancer vaccines which are currently being tested for kidney, ovary, breast, bowel, and lung cancer. But at the time of writing these new vaccines were only available as part of trials, which are the most important way of finding out if new treatments work.

Success in the fight against cancer is shown by a falling rate of death from cancer – that is the number of people dying from cancer per 100,000 population. Until the 1990s the rate of death increased in the USA and Europe and then it steadied or began to fall as a result of improvements in treatment, prevention and screening. More than a quarter of all cancer deaths are caused by lung cancer and smoking but the rate of death from lung cancer is falling, as are deaths from each of the other big killers: breast, bowel and **prostate** cancer.

A person who dies of cancer loses on average fifteen years of life – more years of life than are lost from any other disease including heart disease or strokes. Breast and bowel cancer may strike at a relatively young age and together with cancer in children they are the most important cause of lost years of life. Progress has been made in understanding the link between food and cancer but scientists still have a great deal to learn. Eventually effective ways will be found to prevent cancer as well as better ways of discovering it early and treating it with better targeted drugs that have fewer side effects.

❝If it weren't for cancer I wouldn't have made the changes in my life that gave me the momentum and the courage to do things I never would have done.❞

(Jean Karotkin, Dallas, who had a mastectomy aged 38)

Jane Tomlinson has incurable breast cancer but even so has raised £45,000 for cancer research through her sporting achievements, including a marathon and a triathlon.

Information and advice

A great deal of information about cancer is available on the web. General background information can be obtained and also detailed information about particular types of cancer or particular drugs. Understanding and sympathy can also be obtained from online chat rooms but information obtained from chat rooms should be treated with caution because each case is different.

Contacts in the UK

BACUP
www.cancerbacup.org.uk
This organization provides information and advice to people with cancer in the UK. It provides a free information service run by qualified staff. Free booklets are available by telephone request (020 7696 9003).

Cancer Research UK
www.cancerresearchuk.org
This organization provides useful information about cancer research.

Contacts in Ireland

Irish Cancer Society
www.irishcancer.ie
This society is concerned mainly with delivery of cancer care in Ireland.

Contacts in the USA

The American Cancer Society
www.cancer.org
This organization provides well organized and detailed information about different cancers, cancer treatments and patients' problems.

The Cancer Survivors Network
www.acscsn.org
This is the American Cancer Society's free online support group for cancer survivors and loved ones who share their experiences on message boards.

Oncolink
www.oncolink.upenn.edu
This is a comprehensive information resource on cancer from the University of Pennsylvania, providing in-depth information on most types of cancer.

Candlelighters Childhood Cancer Foundation
www.candlelighters.org
This organization has a mission to educate, support and serve families of children with cancer and survivors of childhood cancer.

Contacts in Australia

Cancer Council of Australia
www.cancer.org.au
This organization provides information about cancer services in Australia and their work with the Australian government to fight disease.

Contacts in Canada

Canadian Cancer Society
www.cancer.ca
This society provides detailed information on specific types of cancer as well as support for cancer patients and their families.

Contacts in New Zealand

New Zealand Cancer Society
www.cancernz.org.nz
This society provides information for people with cancer as well as health professionals.

Other useful contacts

The Association of Cancer Online Resources
www.acor.org
Develops and supports Internet facilities for cancer patients and their families.

Further reading

Good for You! Reducing Your Risk of Developing Cancer, American Cancer Society, 2002. A practical approach to reducing the risk of cancer.

Coming to Terms with Cancer, American Cancer Society, 2002. A–Z reference book giving definitions of more than 1000 words connected with cancer, including drugs.

Cancer in the Family, American Cancer Society, 2002. Helping children cope with a parent's illness.

Childhood Leukaemia: A Guide for Families, Friends and Caregivers (3rd edition), by Nancy Keene; O'Reilly & Associates, 2002. Easy-to-understand guide for families dealing with childhood leukamia.

Childhood Cancer Survivors: A Practical Guide to Your Future, Patient-centred Guides, 2000. Helps children with cancer identify problems and cope.

Fighting Chance: Journeys Through Childhood Cancer, by Harry Connolly, Tom Clancy, Curt I. Civin; Woodholm House, 1998. Contains more than 200 pictures as well as text on the subject of courageous children, strong families and care givers.

You and Leukemia: A Day at a Time, by Lynn S. Baker, Charles G. Roland, Gerald S. Gilchrist; W.B. Saunders, 2002. Explanation of the disease and guide for patients and families.

The Rainbow Feelings of Cancer: A Book for Children Who Have a Loved One with Cancer, by Carrie Martin and Chia Martin; Hohn Press, 2001. A ten-year-old girl writes about her feelings regarding her mother's cancer.

Glossary

acute
used to describe severe conditions which come on suddenly

anaesthesia
bringing about insensitivity to pain using gases or drugs, especially before a surgical operation

biopsy
test involving removal of a small piece of tissue from the body

bone graft
insertion of a piece of bone taken from one part of the body, or from a donor, into another place in the body

bone marrow
soft fatty tissue in the centre of bones that produces all the cells in the blood

cellular pathology
branch of medicine that studies the nature of diseases by examining cells in the laboratory

chemotherapy
treatment of disease with drugs

chronic
used to describe a disease or disorder that persists for a long time

CT scan (computerized tomography)
technique for displaying a cross-section through a human body using X-rays or ultrasound

cyst
abnormal lump or swelling filled with fluid

DNA
deoxyribonucleic acid – the hereditary material, the substance that carries genes in every cell of the body

gamma rays
type of radiation that comes, for example, from the radioactive material cobalt 60

gene
small unit of hereditary material that carries the instruction for building a protein or some other part of an organism

genetic material
another name for DNA

hormone
chemical substance that is released into the body in one place and has an effect in another place

hormone therapy
treatment with hormones or drugs very similar to hormones

immune reaction
reaction of the body's immune system to something in the body such as an infection or growth of malignant tissue

Kaposi's sarcoma
malignant skin tumour, which may occur in association with AIDS but also separately

leukaemia
type of cancer in which white blood cells multiply out of control

lymph
milky fluid containing white blood cells that collects in spaces between cells in the body

lymph ducts
tubes that carry lymph from the tissues back to the blood stream

lymph glands
(also called lymph nodes) small pieces of tissue that are responsible for the immune reactions of the body, so providing defence against infection

malignant
(of cells or tissues) cancerous

mammography
technique that uses X-rays to detect
breast tumours

mastectomy
surgical operation to remove a breast

melanoma
dark coloured mole that contains malignant
tissue – the most serious form of skin cancer

monoclonal antibody
special type of antibody made in the
laboratory, which may be used in treating
cancer

MRI scan (magnetic resonance imaging)
form of imaging which uses high-frequency
radio waves in a strong magnetic field

mutation
change in a gene

non-Hodgkin's lymphoma
any cancer of lymph tissue other than
Hodgkin's lymphoma (a type of cancer
involving the lymph glands)

non-melanoma skin cancer
any type of skin cancer other than melanoma

PET scan (positron emission tomography)
form of imaging used especially for scanning
the brain

prostate
gland located under the bladder in men,
which makes the fluid part of semen

radioactive implant
small piece of material, such as wire, which
is inserted into a tumour and produces
radioactivity that kills off surrounding cells

radiotherapy
treatment with X-rays or other types of
radiation

remission
temporary reduction in severity of disease

sarcoma
cancer of connective tissue, that is the tissue
which surrounds organs and holds different parts
of the body together

screening test
test to find out if someone has a cancer in their
body that they do not know about

sexually transmitted disease
disease which infects someone as a result of
sexual intercourse or other sexual activity

sputum
mixture of saliva and mucus coughed up from the
respiratory tract

stem cells
cells present in many tissues of the body that
give rise to more specialized cells typical of a
particular tissue

thyroid gland
gland located in the front of the neck that
regulates the body's energy level

transfusion
transfer of blood or other fluid into a person's
body

tumour
usually refers to a lump or piece of tissue that is
malignant, but more strictly means a swelling
that may be malignant (cancerous) or benign
(not malignant)

ultrasound
sound which cannot be heard by the human ear,
used in medicine to produce images of internal
parts of the body

white blood cells
cells in the blood that defend the body against
infection

Index

Titles in the *Need to Know* series include:

Need to Know
ADHD
Philippa Pigache

Hardback   0 431 18840 8

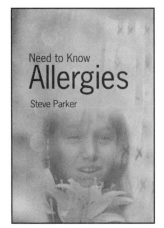

Need to Know
Allergies
Steve Parker

Hardback   0 431 09760 7

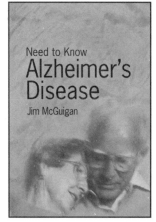

Need to Know
Alzheimer's Disease
Jim McGuigan

Hardback   0 431 18841 6

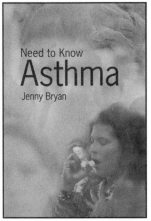

Need to Know
Asthma
Jenny Bryan

Hardback   0 431 09761 5

Need to Know
Cancer
Oliver Gillie

Hardback   0 431 18842 4

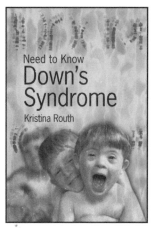

Need to Know
Down's Syndrome
Kristina Routh

Hardback   0 431 18843 2

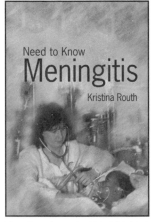

Need to Know
Meningitis
Kristina Routh

Hardback   0 431 18844 0

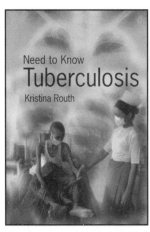

Need to Know
Tuberculosis
Kristina Routh

Hardback   0 431 18845 9

Find out about the other titles in this series on our website www.heinemann.co.uk/library